Krystal...

Thank you so much for your kindness and continuous support....

It is more very much appreciated...

Remain blessed and beautiful

Jah X-El

© 2009 Marlon J. McGowan

Published by Jah X-El Publications

Edited by Beatrice M. Haywood

Printed in the United States of America

WORDS OF GRATITUDE

My gift which is the ability to take thoughts and express them in words then structure those words into what is manifested as poetry, would NOT be in existence without God & my Mama, Doris Jean McGowan.
(God has you now Ma... I KNOW you're well!!!)

Thank you BOTH immeasurably!!!

I love you BOTH infinitely!!!

Jah X-El

TABLE OF CONTENT

Chapter IV

Spiritually Speaking...

"A Prayer We All Have In Common"
"Jah's Prayer For Deliverance"
"Losing Her Religion"
"Jah's Prayer For Release"
"For Once She Prays"

Chapter V

There's Lesson's In Losing...

"Just Tired"
"Some Days Are Better Than Others"
"For Whatever Reason"
"Soul Exposed"
"I Miss You"
"The First Time"
"4 Minutes"

Chapter VI

Start To Stop...

"Days Like This"
"Can I Have A Few Minutes Of Your Time Please?"
"Stop The Dance"

Chapter VII

Eye / I Empathize, Encourage, and Empower...

"Fellow Men"
"!!!!!NEWFLASH!!!!!"
"My Apology" (For men who can't do it)
"!!!!!NEWFLASH Part 2!!!!!" (The confessions of the bad black man)
"You Will Survive"

Jah'isms

Inspirational Poems for Women

"Allow Me To Introduce Myself"

These words you read
are **NOT** poetry...

Just my narration
of the things
that I feel, think, experience, believe, and see...

This is about **ME** and a glimpse into the womb of my mind where ideas aren't
always conceived immaculately, because influence comes in many forms
constantly

Both internally and externally...

But I share with you my mentality...

I remove my mask and strip naked and allow you to see

JAH

My pen or keyboard acting as midwife in my attempt to birth and give life to my
thoughts and make them reality...

Living and breathing...

Constantly growing and changing...

Going through phases,
just as you and I,
because in all actuality
life is truly the poetry
in motion
perpetuated by forces seen and unseen...

Heard and unheard...

Felt and not felt...

I am JAH

And my new lines and concepts are added continuously as life changes constantly...

Molding, weakening, breaking, rebuilding, strengthening, and shaping...

JAH

And at times I am struck with moments of clarity like the thought that I am YOU and YOU are...

JAH

Everything is connected to everything so we are "WE"...

A patchwork quilt made with different swatches of fabric of many different colors, patterns, and textures that look nice individually, but sewn together, create a work of art that was crafted beautifully and masterfully...

I told you...

I am YOU and YOU are...

JAH

See, life is about connection of all things from mental to physical to spiritual...

The trinity of life that exists in and around us but is often ignored because somewhere between our inception and conception we lost our sense of connectivity...

Walking around
in the ambiguity of individuality...

Assuming that it IS all about us personally...

NEVER stopping to notice the cause and effect or the cause and affect that link us all non-physically...

Yet we exchange vibes and energy...

Sometime's purposefully...

Sometime's inadvertently...

Our eyes are wide shut usually...

Often too disconnected from self to appreciate the exchange and the connection to our surroundings...

But for a *moment...*

Then all of a sudden I was wide-awake and I saw the world differently...

I am Jah

SO I FIGHT SLEEP!!!

...mentally...

Staying conscious by attempting to wake you and make you think...

Provoking and evoking enlightenment so that you can join me because from where I stand it can get lonely, so I share myself with you so you can get to know me...

Allow me to introduce myself...

I AM JAH

Let's connect...

Chapter I

I Understand...

"If Only He Could" (A man thinking as woman)

If only he could comprehend
the makings of whom I am.

To hear...

Without speaking, understand
With ears open to thoughts feminine
Tolerate effeminate quips
Comprehending a woman's aural senses are important

To see...

Beyond a sensual silhouette
Amalgamate our imagination
Sight past Venus visions
Comprise **US** into a compilation

To touch...

Deeply, feeling not just the delicate
Make intricate contact, not feel me complicate
My emotions, finger them with no neglect
Omit **NOTHING** adjacent to mentally caressing me with respect

To taste...

Cycles change sanity...Infallible
But I ask that you become a connoisseur of Queen cuisine
Hungrily; Savor faults that are unpalatable
Monthly sours create tears, but manifest wisdom invaluable

To live...

HE is NOT without **SHE**, breathe my essence
Inhale **WOMAN**, exhale my blessings
Become a scholar of femininity, embrace my lessons
My love is your strength, an immeasurable power without question

If only "**WE**" could comprehend,
the makings of who women are...

"The Day He Left You" (Or did you leave him???)

He pressed you against the wall

Your nails sank deep into his chest

His back

His hands slipped around your waist

Your neck

(YOUR NECK!?)

His hands around your neck

Holding you

Choking you

"Why?"

"What did I do this time?"

(THIS TIME?!?)

You struggle to breath
as you feel yourself
losing this battle

"I CAN'T BREATH!"

...You cough...

He whispers that he loves you

....You **SCREAM**...

He shouts that he loved you

(HE LOVED YOU?)

But his hands **NEVER** left your neck

It was just an argument

A disagreement

A minor misunderstanding

"*You LOVED me!?*"

That's really all you heard

But his hands **NEVER** left your neck

And his grip is getting tighter

But you've been through this before

And he **NEVER** said that **he LOVED** you before

Not like that, in the past tense

As if he were leaving you

"*He LOVED me?*"

....You gag...

His grip tightens

....You gasp...

He apologizes

"O.k., everything is going to be alright now"

...You think...

Because his hands never leave your neck

You mumble; "*You said the last time we went through this, THIS won't happen again?*"

He says; "**This is different, you REALLY hurt me this time!**"

(WHAT!?!)

This is just an **ARGUMENT**!

A **DISAGREEMENT**!

A minor **MISUNDERSTANDING**!

You all **ALWAYS** go through this
but the *last* time you went through this
you said will be the **LAST** time you all go through this
because the next time you go through this
may be your **LAST TIME** going through this

THIS may be your ***LAST TIME*** going through this

Maybe you won't make it to **NEXT** time

Because his hands never left your neck

And now your vision is blurry

Your breathing is shallow

It's starting to get dark

"But we argue all the time
then we make up;
That's when the love is good"

He agrees
He loves that make up sex

He loves "*IT*" when you're mad

Because he likes it rough

But his hands are **STILL** wrapped around your neck

Every other day these arguments

These disagreements

These minor misunderstandings

This **ABUSE**!

Ignored by you
but seen by many
as just what it is

!!!ABUSE!!!

But it continues without fail

As you live in denial

And go through this hell

Your love
You give unconditionally

Your heart

You give unconditionally

"I LOVE YOU!"

He says he wants it no more

"Why?"

?????????????????????????????

(WHY!?!)

He says you're not going to do to anyone else what you did to him

"WHAT???"

"BUT I LOVE YOU!!!!!"

He responds by saying that he loved you

"You LOVED me?"

Maybe,
you think,
as you settle into the darkness,
that it's just your time to go...

(!!!WOW!!!)

"The Night He Said These Words To You"

"I WILL STOP BREATHING BEFORE I EVER HURT YOU"

Do you remember the night he said those words to you?

He said he **NEVER** loved anyone the way he love you, and
that he would stop breathing before he ever hurt you

You had just made love to him

You were lying against his chest

He asked why you were crying when he felt your tears drop

At first you couldn't answer

You don't know why you were crying

"**DID I HURT YOU**", he asked, concerned that he
he may have not been gentle enough with you

"*No*", you said, as you attempted to assure him

It wasn't physical pain you were feeling

What you felt was emotional

SO emotional!

Because you were scared

Terrified actually

You had **NEVER** loved anyone the way you loved him

And you were afraid that he wasn't at that same point
as far as how he felt for you, regardless of his acts

Or rather his "**PERFORMANCE**"

You realize "*IT'S*" good...No, it's beyond that...**NO ONE**
else **EVER** caused your body to go through those
shakes and shivers...**EVER!**

But you know you have to leave that bed sometime

Then what?

You expressed your fear...

That you were afraid that he got what he wanted; to
be truthful, **ALWAYS** get what he wants

...(Those **DAMN** shakes and shivers!)...

So he no longer has a need for you beyond
the bedroom, or the occasional outing

You **FINALLY** got the courage to say those words

And then

He paused

And told you to look at him

And when you couldn't

He took your face in his hands and said

I WILL STOP BREATHING BEFORE I EVER HURT YOU

You believed him

In that moment, if he would've told you the sun was
a shade of green plaid, you would've believed him

You made love to him again

..."*These **DAMN** shakes!*"...

And *again*

..."*These **DAMN** shivers!!!!*"...

Until you couldn't anymore

Then you slept

The sleep only lovers sleep

Satisfied
Sated
Content

In love

Now

Nine months later

As you lay in a hospital room

Alone

With only your child's breathing to be heard

You wonder

Is he **STILL** breathing!?!?

Chapter II

Confusion Sets In...

"Mistreated" (The twisted thinking)

Wasted your time
in trouble before

That nigga that
came pounding
on your door

Called you bitches,
rats, and whores

That foolish love
you had, you're
hoping not to
have anymore

You hated him
but you had
felt that you
were trapped

Held

Imprisoned

Incarcerated

Grown
but
kidnapped

Thinking of ways
to get away

Or get back
at his foolish crap

You try to stay away for days before your whole world snaps

Everyone tells
you that he's
NO good

But everyone
says to him,
that ***YOU TOO***
live fowl

You reply,

"Whatever!!!
I wanna get away
BELIEVE *me, but*
I just don't
know how?"

But you said it
smirking, and
with a sly smile

A relationship
based on sex

And you thought
his dick was
NO GOOD anyway

And he thought
your pussy
was **BLEW OUT**

And you're **BOTH**
trying to hurt each
other in **ANY** way

He tries to change your life by saying,

"Baby, your childhood
friends are
really your enemies"

And you saying
to him about
his friends,

"Baby, they aren't who they pretend to be"

Silly YOU

You're trying to
keep him to yourself

Keep him trapped
tightly in your grasp

Just like he
has **Silly YOU**

So he calls
you every minute
to assure you
that he's not
sliding in the grass

But the whole
time **YOU** were
also being a snake

Creeping

Any time you
thought he
was sleeping

So this is
your way of
mistreating
him for being
mistreated

Twisted Thinking

"It takes A Strong Woman" (Truth misunderstood)

It takes a strong woman
to be in love with a man
when she *knows* he's
NOT treating her right

(It does???)

It takes a strong woman
to **NOT** confront her
man when he *didn't*
come home last night

(Or a woman who'll tolerate anything...)

It takes a strong woman
to close her eyes
and **NOT** see what is
in front of her face

(Yeah, RIGHT!!!)

It takes a strong woman
to *keep up* her man's
lies when **ANOTHER**
woman is taking her place

(Uh huh)

It takes a strong woman
to sacrifice *her own*
happiness just to make
her house a home

(You can believe that if you want to)

It takes a strong woman
to *live* with a cheating man

INSTEAD OF LIVING ALONE

(I hope that none of *YOU* have this type of strength)

"Slick Talker" (You better watch out!!!)

I want to know you

EVERYTHING about you

I want to go beyond myself and learn you

In and out

All the way thru

Do crazy, spontaneous ass shit for you

Be something like a best friend to you

Be someone you can lean on and confide in for you

The one who understands you no matter what's going on with you

That's all I want to do for you

...I'm lying...

I **ALSO** want to be a sidekick for you

Make you feel like you bleed greatness

Do what I was created to do for you

To **SUPPORT** you

I want to know the things that make you laugh
so I can bring pleasure and delight into your life for you

I want to know the things that make you
tick so I can avoid bringing rage into your
atmosphere...

Your stratosphere...

Baby, into your **WORLD**

That's all I want to do for you

...I'm lying...

Because I also want to know your fears
and weaknesses so I can provide courage and
build you up and make you stronger

And you should know I would
NEVER use negativity against you

I want to be considered that positive vibe in your
life that brings ecstasy and wealth to you

Help you live out all your dreams with you

I want to make you feel like you're the greatest
thing that ever walked the earth's surface
because baby you're worth it

You think I'm lying?

I want to be the one you want to talk to

The one who you can pour your soul and **ALL** your
deepest intimate thoughts and secrets into

You know, **YOUR PERSONAL DIARY** for you

...Dig...

I have an idea

We can play "**Sex and the City**" and I can get
dressed up and look **SO** handsome for you

I can be **Mr. Big** and you be *Carrie*

And I'll do anything that makes you happy

...For you...

I'll give delirious dick

Sex you senseless for you

Give you crazy climaxes

I have psychotic penis for you

*I'm **NOT** lying about **THAT***

But I can also show you the respect you honestly deserve

Make you feel like a woman should feel

You know, be there for you whenever you need me
like a 24-hour ATM machine for you

Baby you can withdraw what
you need from me **ANYTIME**

I want to be the artist and make you
into a beautiful masterpiece for you

I want to help build you up to the
LADY you're destined to be for you

I'll be your hype man, something
like a number one fan for you

I just want to carry your burdens during hard
and heavy times and make life easier for you

Believe me

I'll ask **GOD** to give me the strength to
carry you on my shoulders when you're weak

And when you feel that you've messed up,
I want to be the one who dusts your
shoulders off and get you back on your feet

...For you...

I want the goodness in my heart
to inspire you to bloom into the beautiful
rose-of-a-woman you're meant to be

I want to know what makes you *forever smile*
so I can grant happiness **ALWAYS** for you

Forget about all these other *man-fools*

All my heart desires to do is
to be there **ONLY** for **YOU**

*I'm **NOT** lying*

I just want to finish
doing **ME** with *your help* **FIRST**

But **TRUST ME**, it's for *YOU*

Chapter III

Decisions...

"Loving Him"

She has been
victimized by his
masculine touch

Hypnotized by
his mesmerizing
words

**Loving him is
as HARD as
it is *easy***

Loathing him
is an
unnatural response

A defense mechanism
NECESSITATED by
his treachery

He is as
POWERFUL as
he is *weak*

He can be as
warm and
gentle as he is
cold and **callous**

He is a
paradoxical parasite

Eating away
at her soul

While stimulating
her flesh

He sends her
through unnecessary
emotional windfalls

**Loving him is
like being
addicted to drugs**

When she's on
that high **NOTHING
ELSE** seems to
matter except
how good he
makes her feel

She gets that addictive rush

And when she
comes crashing down
she's left strung
out on misery

Losing **ALL** sight
of herself

Finding herself
begging and
pleading

For his attention

For his acceptance

For his praise

Begging and
pleading for
him **NEVER** to
leave her again

**Loving him has
taken its toll**

It has
accelerated
her days

Making her appear
much older than
her years portray

Building him up
should never
tear her down

**Loving him
should never result
in hating herself**

Now her self
esteem has been
demolished with
the ruins being
thrown into a
bottomless pit
which seemingly
falls below the
depths of hell level

She's tired of
being *broken
into fractions*
in order to *make
him feel whole*

The numbers in
those calculations
NO LONGER add
up correctly

Not to mention
her measurements
being constantly mishandled

Lowering herself
to suit his standards

His lies twisting
her brain as
well as his
tongue so his
speeches are
in rambles

Childish man,
mannish boy,
male of scandals

When your eyes
are wide open
you see that
the man he
portrayed himself
to be is
actually crumbling
to shambles

**Loving him is like
being born again**

Only to endure
a more
excruciating demise

NO LONGER will
she allow herself
to be victimized

By his
infidelities,
insecurities
and lies

The spell
he once had
cast between
her thighs

With his

mediocre
"rise"

Has since
been broken

She can **NO LONGER**

Justify her
love while
wishing to
crucify her lover

Meaningless words
are **NO**
LONGER hypnotic

When **LOATHING**
him comes as
naturally as *loving*
him then **LEAVING**
him is the
ONLY thing left
for her to do

"She Cries Out"

She says she's tired of these disrespecting boys...

Silly acting boys...

The wanna be 50 Cent boys...

The one that don't hold your hand when he with his
boys because he's scared they might call him weak, boy...

The one that get with you just because he think he's gonna "*beat*", boy...

She said she can't stand one that is so controlling and self-conscious
to the point you can't go anywhere without him, boy...

The one that don't call you back when you called his ass about 10 times, boy...

She says she need a
respecting man...

A smart about the relationship, man...

A confident man that is satisfied with his self, and if he's not
he tries to improve himself, man...

The one that is proud of his relationship and doesn't care who knows it, man...

The one that get with you not only for your body but personality and soul, man...

A man that call you first and ask how your day been, man...

She says she wants to love a man that doesn't get jealous
because another man is looking at you, man...

The one who caters to you each night, and he is positive
and secure you won't leave him, man...

ATTENTION!

ATTENTION!!

ATTENTION!!!

She cries out that if anybody find a man like that, please come find her because she'll be the one still with the disrespecting, funny acting, self-conscious boy, waiting for him to turn from a boy to a man, *wanna-be-man*, boy...

"What About "Him"???"

You **knew** what
the two of
you were doing
was **WRONG**...

But when your
bodies connected, it
just **felt so right**...

See, when **he**
touches you in
all the right
places, you feel
this power fall
over you
like voodoo...

But when "*he*"
touches you, that
feeling **ISN'T** there...

You see, "*he*"
satisfies you
emotionally
and *mentally*...

But **he** satisfies
you **physically**
and **sexually**...

When you lay
alone in your
bed, you can
feel **his** strong
hands caressing
your body...

You can feel

his tongue touch
your spine...

You can feel
him slowly
entering and
searching for
your soul...

You **NEVER**
meant for this
to go this far
but **he** trapped
you in his
maze of lust
and now you
CAN'T get out...

Oh, I know,
what you two
do feels good
in **EVERY** way
but you're **ONLY**
HURTING YOURSELVES...

You can't have
him the way
you want **him**
and **HE CAN'T**
HAVE YOU...

So is this a
waste of you
all's time?

Or is this
your destiny?

To please and be pleased?

Was it meant

for **him** to
be addicted to
how you
feel inside?

Was it meant
for you
to let **him**?

These are the
questions you
ponder on
EVERYDAY
when you
think of **him**...

When you think
of being together...

You don't want
to put an end
to you all's
little rendezvous,
so now you want
to ask **him**
to make it
something more...

Secret Lovers No More...

My **ONLY** question to you is...

What about "*him*"?????

"Mr. What If"

He's the one you made love to...

(Whether you wanted to or not)

In a dream...

*(That you wish would **CONTINUOUSLY** come true)*

Or in reality...

*(Because to cum like that should be something experienced in **REAL** life!)*

The one who slips into your thoughts when you're alone...

(The first sign that you're whipped)

Or with someone else...

*(The **CONFIRMATION** that you're whipped!)*

He's the one you yearn for...

(Like a crack head for rocks)

The one you let get away...

(Damn! If you would've just let him do.... Or maybe if you did....)

The one whom you reminisce about past affections...

(Uh, Oh.....)

The man you think of one-day feeling clear reflections of his love...

*(**NOW** it's serious!)*

He makes you laugh when the world's cruelty makes you cry...

(Oh.....)

When everyone else only sees the style of your hair...

(Lord.....)

The make-up on your face...

(PLEASE!)

The build of your body...

(Don't)

He knows your mind...

(Let)

Feels your spirit...

(Me)

And sees your soul...

(Do)

Underneath it all...

(This)

He's the friend that's MORE than a friend...

(To)

The crush...

(Myself)

The old flame that continues burning within you...

(Again!!!)

The man who you would...

*(Fuck it! **I AM!**)*

If you could...
(I can accept a physical relationship)

But you won't...

*(**DAMN**! Why should I **JUST** have the dick!? But it **IS** good!)*

Because for some reason, you can't...

*(You **KNOW** why!)*

But what if "**Mr. What If**" was yours?

(Hmmm???)

Reminder

Re-introduction...

"I Am Jah"

I am **NOT** easy

NOT like *him*

I am Jah

I like to reside in your mind

Sit on the tips of your lips

My name pour forth from your mouth

Jah

In rhythmic patterns you say it

J

A

H

I coerce you into confessing every sin committed in the name of love

Reveal yourself to **ME**!

Jah

Mentally, I push you to the limit of your academic cliff

I tip toe to the back of your soul undetected
and push you into a pulsating
linguistic expedition
beyond your mediocre conversation with past men evoking all the mind arousal and mental
orgasms
you can stand

just by

saying

my

name

JAH

No need to thank me...

The pleasure was **ALL** mine!

Chapter IV

Spiritually Speaking...

"A Prayer We All Have In Common"

I pray for a love that is unconditional,
spiritually sound, and solid...

A love in which we are connected on four levels and not just three...

I pray for a love that when we come together as one it's more than physical,
even though that *is* how we express ourselves sometimes...

A lasting love that only happens when
two complete people find each other...

I pray for a lover that's my best friend...

A lover that's easy to communicate with, has soft touches,
gentle caresses, and warm words...

A lover that is strong, but sensitive
hard, yet supple, like **ME**...

One not afraid to cry in front of, or with me, as I am with her...

I pray for a lover with a brilliant mind, but not overbearing...

Strong, yet soft hands that feel like silk against my skin...

With kisses that feel like whispering winds...

Light and velvety soft...

I wonder will God bring my prayer to a reality
when He blesses me with you???

"Jah's Prayer For Deliverance"

In an
unsaved life

Sometimes
days appear
only as nights

When spiritually
is lost in the
abyss of darkness
we can **NEVER**
find the lights

The atmosphere
seems thicker
than quicksand
and blacker than
a million midnights

I was unable
to see my
own hand or
so much as its silhouette in
front of my face

I was confused,
off-balanced
and discouraged,
allowing deception
to impede my
once quick pace

My mind
became clouded,
vision shrouded

I felt left was
all that's left,
cause right just
didn't seem right

I felt lacerated,
contused, bleeding

and stumbling
helplessly devoid
of sight or insight

I questioned
if the proverbial
towel should
be thrown in,
or perhaps just
bandage the
wounds and
continue to fight

My entire directive,
appeared deceptive,

It became imperative
for me to sever
the connective of
the impious collective

Now, because of
my Christian living,
I'm seeming what
others perceive as
"funny acting"
and overprotective

With judgments selective

But I'll continue
persevering with a
righteous perspective

In search of
His peaceful perfection

Not ephemeral affection

Or some meaningless
satisfaction for
my seminal erection

Or superficial connection

Instead, I **KNOW**
I'm in desperate
need of **His** protection

His Fatherly correction

His heavenly direction

Spirituality which will
dispel my own will and
insubordinate insurrection

His love is
empowering with
the strength to
avoid those solely
pulchritudinous,
ironically
atrocious within

His love eradicates
the purposeful
ill-fated plans
of the evil
one, who
must reluctantly
now rescind

He restores faith
completely, solid
from becoming
simply deliquesce

We're not here
on earth to
stay, but elevate
your minds
spiritually while
remaining grounded
with only
God to impress

He is before
me, evil one
behind me, the
once dim way
is now clear

All belligerent,
possessive, or
pugnacious must

also reversely
retreat to
the rear

I'm feeling like
a celebration is
in order, while
reflecting back
on those times

Once scraping
and scrounging
for the devil's
pennies profusely,
ignoring God's
valuable and
devoted dimes

I'll be exceptionally
blessed with
the dime He
places by
my side, while
continuing to
allow **Him** to
encourage and lead

Digesting knowledge
as if food, the
light shines bright,
for God grants
the ability for
me and **ALL**
to succeed!!!

Losing Her Religion

She once had
an affair
with Jesus

That was when
she first met
her current man

Coincidentally, that
was also during
the time when
her mouth and
eyes were regularly
swollen shut

That relationship
was kept
quite hush-hush

Afraid that her
current man
would find
out and no
"Hail Mary's" or
"Hallelujahs"
could save
her butt from
being bust

For him, she
lost her religion

No when she's
with her current
man, his voice
beats at her
wildly, like his

fist sometimes
did, with the
promise of a fake,
materialistic heaven
complete with
wings that would
be tattooed onto
her shoulder bones

She preferred false
words from a
false-prophet-of-a-man
as opposed to the
redeeming rhetoric
of Jesus

She suffocated
under the scrutinizing
red light of
her current man's
eternal flame of
anger and abuse
as opposed to
breathing in the
white glow of
Jesus' glorious joy
and happiness

She no longer
believed in a
man nailed on
a cross, but
she **NEEDED** to

She **NEEDED** to
cross back into
a divine state
of mind so
she can stop
believing in
a man who

just wanted
to nail her

She kept waiting
to be touched
by an angel,
to be swept
up in the
arms of a man
who was spiritual
and walked
in faithfulness

She no longer
wanted to be
touched by her
current man, a
devil incarnate
whom held her
in evil arms
and walked in
the ways of
the wicked

So she dumped
her current man,
a man who
never lovingly
held her, but
slapped her with
the palms of his
hands claiming
he does it
out of love

She gained the
courage to leave
him to elope
with a man
who had holes
in the palms
of his hands

because he
DID love her

A marriage of
help, but it
was what she
needed from
a savior

Saved

Once lost,
but now found

"Jah's Prayer For Release"

You have carried
me in your arms
along a journey
of paradise lost...

Longing to
be found...

Longing to see
the rainbow for
its true colors...

Hear my cry
and speak to me...

You, who was
wrought with the
burdens of us all...

You, whose blood
spilled into every
valley of the earth
as darkness befell...

The Son, who
embodied the
sun to make
you OUR daylight
amidst the night....

You, who has
shown me the
Promised Land
as you did Moses...

Behold, I am
NO Moses...

I am Jah

Acting instead
as Joshua...

Wrapped up in

many moments
of freeing myself
and your people
from these
wretched woes
with my poetry...

These burdens I
carry when I try
to express their
ailing thoughts
in poetic verse...

Why can't
I always
release them???

I am engulfed
in iniquity on
this day and
cannot find the
strength to
write or pray...

There are only
familiar words
to write and say,
yet again,
as so many
times before...

Can you
forgive me?

You are the
tutor, I am
the student

Yet why
the difficulty
in learning?

Because I **STILL**
act of my
own will and
not **YOURS**!!!

By your blood

I was saved...

By your beaten
flesh was
I healed...

Yet, at times,
I dishonor
your memory...

Periodically, with
my words, actions,
and deeds, I
continue to
drive the nails
into your hands
and feet further
and further with
each transgression...

Again, oh Lord,
hear my cry and
speak to me...

Free me from
this feeling of
guilt, shame, and
hopelessness when
I can't scribe
the words to
help others, for
I torment myself...

Just as you
were tormented,
yet you stood
so firmly planted
to the ground...

I say now,
Oh Lord,
for all that
you've done..

I **WILL** live
for you,
breathe for
you, and

if need be...

Even **DIE**
for you!!!!!

For you are
the reason I
live, it is
your breath
that sustains
my life, and
as I know
now, will
NEVER have
to spiritually
die because
of you...

For I realize
now that you
died so I
wouldn't have to...

THANK YOU
my Lord for
speaking to
me just now...

This moment is
the moment I
start **LIVING
FOR RELEASE**!

"For Once She Prays"

For Once She Prays

(As she lay awake in his arms)

"Let him be the one to live up to his words"

She Prays

*"Not just empty promises of a
lustful boy that are filled with
dreams that are fit for a little girl,
or a woman with the mind of one"*

She Prays

*"Let him be the **MAN** he says he is,
with the **ACTIONS** to back his words,
and has my best interest at heart"*

She Prays

*"Make him understand that I'm a
good woman who's been hurt before,
therefore he'll have the patience and
tolerance to help me thru these issues
as opposed to faulting me for having
them, because one more bad
relationship could be the last straw"*

She Prays

*"Let him see beyond my breasts,
hips and thighs, and see the
beautiful woman that lives inside"*

She Prays

*"Let him love me not only for
my body, but also my mind"*

She Prays

*"If he **TRULY** is the man for me
then everything I've prayed for,
he will **ALREADY** know"*

Chapter V

There's Lessons In Losing...

"Just Tired"

This hand grows weary of being held so tightly...
You act as if you will never let it go...

Funny, how mind and body disagree...
And in the chaos, you do not know...

This heart is tired of waiting for an answer...
It has been screaming for attention for too long...

Now even when the promise is forever, this heart has difficulty holding on...

These dreams are tired of being put on hold....
Waiting for you to grow into your role...

There is nothing like time being wasted, especially when the body is growing old...

This body is tired of wanting...
Hoping that the touch will be there...

Cold sheets remind me of the time before you...
Way before I was strong enough to care...

These tears are tired of falling
they never do reach their end...

The path they made upon my cheeks reminds me of when I lost my friend...

"Some Days Are Better Than Others"

Some days are better than others

Sometimes it's hard for you to breathe

Sometimes it's hard for you to make it through the day since, you think,

"There's no him, and without him, there's no me."

Some days you just smile

You just refuse to be depressed and sad

Other times the silence just gets to you from the loneliness you now have

Sometimes you can't stop laughing

Other times you just feel so alone

So desperate to hear his voice

Too scared to pick up the phone

Wondering if this is for the best?

Wondering what did you learn?

What was the lesson taught?

How about how not to get your heart burned???

But some days are better than others

It's the good memories that keep you, and the illusion of *you and he*, once again being "**US**", alive

In your heart and mind your disillusions have him captured on the days your heart doesn't cry

You tell yourself

"Be strong!!!"

"Everything will be okay!!!"

Yet, without him in your life, sometimes it takes a few ounces more
than a tremendous effort just to make it through the day

Just wish he could understand

Just wish you could see him again

You just miss the way the two of you were

You just miss your man

But some days are better than others

And you say to yourself, *"For once, now I'm free!"*

But all the while you're really thinking,

"I would give nearly anything just to have him back in love with me!"

But *some days* **ARE** better than others

And I guess *today* just **ISN'T** one of those days

"For Whatever Reason"

For whatever reason

Someone finds you

Someone holds you

Someone wants you

Someone loves you

Sweet invitations

Dark sensations

Fierce temptations

Probing examinations

Intimate relations

Stimulating pulsations

Aware of the dangers

You let yourself fall

Let yourself need

Let yourself trust

Your mind is stolen

Your heart is taken

All the while drowning

In a black sea of fantasy

Then the music changes

Laughter melts into searing tears

Every touch leaves a scar

No longer speaking the same language

No longer hearing the same words

No longer wanting the same things

The final confrontation
to a blackened destination
leaves complete devastation
and abundant aggravation

An inconsolable revelation
without justification

For whatever reason

Someone loses

Someone lets go

Someone wants something else

Someone is no longer in love

Someone walks away

"Soul Exposed"

Uncertainty,
doubtful,
skeptical,
unsure,
suspicious,
variable,
unsteady,
ambiguous,
and unsettled

ALL describe my
feelings right now

Painful,
aching,
bitter,
grievous,
injured,
damaged,
blemished,
tarnished,
outraged,
anguished,
misery,
and strife

You hurt me,
after I allowed
you into my life

Freely,
willingly,
wittingly,
hesitant
yet, voluntarily

I permitted you into
this special place

Specifically,
individually,
particularly,
powerfully,
influentially,
imperatively,
substantially,
and significantly
dwelling within
my soul

And I
was helplessly,
hopelessly

Devolving,
dropping,
descending,
sinking,
slumping,
declining,
and surrendering

That safeguarded
place I placed
into your dominion

Consenting to
something
new,
different,
fresh,
non-existent,
unfamiliar,
innovative,
variant,
and unlike
ANYTHING
I have
ever experienced!!!

Savored,

tasted,
felt,
practiced,
pursued,
employed,
implemented,
sensed,
and perceived

...**YOU**...

are at the very
center of my
existence,
my core,
my being,
my focus,
my essence,
my fortitude,
my very spirit...

Although unsure of
the consequences

Significance,
importance,
outcome,
aftermath,
tangible,
and fruits

I **STILL**
welcomed the
change into
my life

Now I sit
here in such
unimpeded solitude
feeling my
soul is exposed

Unobstructed,
uncovered,
unprotected,
public,
unrestricted,
unoccupied,
undiscovered,
and vulnerable

For **ALL** the
world to see

The me...

The **REAL** me

The me I wanted
YOU to see!!!

Behold,
conceive,
anticipate,
envision,
observe,
comprehend,
and grasp

Enveloping everything
you notice

Fencing,
hedging,
protecting,
enclosing,
investing,
unwrapping,
besieging,
and encompassing

The once foreign
element that

YOU uncovered

Revealing,
displaying,
disclosing,
unmasking
to even myself

Yet **YOU** witnessed
it for yourself!!!

You're **NOT** sure,
when I'm **SO** sure
about this thing

You said you
were, so I bought
a wedding ring

You're **NOT**
serious; You're still
stuck on him

You hurt my
feelings, and
once more
I'm alone!

MAD!!

FRUSTRATED!!!

And ready to
RE-BUILD that
once crumbling
wall of protection

Guarded,
defended,
secured,
protected,
safeguarded,

shielded,
unharmed,
and partitioned

I sit here

Independently

Unaccompanied

Abandoned

Rebuilding that
once crumbling
fence of shelter

Delighted,
doting,
passionately,
adoring,
devoted,
amorously, and
anxiously willing

To take you back

Yet

I sit here

Frantic

Indignant

Delirious

Brick after brick,
recovering,
restoring,
reconstructing,
that barrier that
once protected

this heart of mine

Feeling silly,
betrayed,
crossed,
misguided,
unveiled,
tricked,
bluffed,
deceived,
and duped

Into believing
the words you
said were true

I'm sitting here

Defeated

Baffled

Enraged

Layer upon layer,
returning,
replacing,
reintroducing my
crushed heart back
to its earliest place
of masked defense

NEVER to expose
my soul again!!!

" I Miss You "

Appreciation goes undetected

Waking moments are often neglected

Until someone comes along

Once here, now gone

The way they laugh

The way they sneezed

...Silly Me...

Penning and reminiscing

Remembering how two negatives became
a positive

How your bad habits became
an appreciated memory

A smile on the face

A passing embrace

...Cherished now...

What was once neglected
is now appreciated

...Left reflecting...

Words like "**I love you**" stain
your brain and stagnate your progression

One should cherish each moment

No one is promised "**The Next Day**"

Cherish the life that we
are given

First time speaking

might be the last time to say
whatever you think you *should*
say now that *they're here* that
you **WON'T** be able to say when
they're gone and it's **TOO LATE** to say

As for me, I sometimes desire to relive the past

Changing everything up until the point
where I saw you last

I would have held you longer

I miss you

Held you stronger

I MISS YOU

Penning and reminiscing

"I Love "YOU""

Your memory

Staining my brain

Your memory

Stagnating my progression

Penning and reminiscing

Now I hold on to lasting impressions

Conversations, letters, and facial
expressions

...Reflecting...

A time of happiness
is deeply implanted

I wish I
never took that period of
time for granted

I miss you

"The First Time"

The first phone call

The first conversation

The right moment

The first time your voices connected

The right time

The first date

Not wanting it to end

Driving home

He is consuming your thoughts

The first realization

A revelation

Still remembering his presence

The first time hours passed

And passed

Choosing his voice over much needed sleep

The first time comprehending that you consume this man too

His thoughts

His heart

The first time you smelled his cologne

Delicious

Wondering what scent is that?

The first time he held you

He's strong

Masculine

The first time you danced with him

The first time you looked into his eyes

The first time he touched you

The first time he made you laugh

The first time he made love to you

The first orgasm

The first time you realized that you missed him

The first time you realized that somehow

Someway

You wanted to feel
the first time **AGAIN**

Because you're *now* realizing for *the first time* that he's **REALLY** gone

"4 Minutes"

What happens when you ignore a woman's silent cries?

Tears asking for more, that simply go unheard

(*Baby, **PLEASE**! Let me talk to you!*)

Covering with lies to disguise the truth a man **CAN'T** accept

(*She's gone...*)

Regrets; These things follow us so long

Well after the person has left and gone

And a man is left staring at the door, wondering

(*I didn't appreciate her when I had her...*)

"I don't know what it was???
I could blame it on a thousand things but I just wasn't listening
with all the clutter of the real world I couldn't avoid
I just couldn't hear her.

Too much noise in the background.

I know there was a void and I tried to cover substance with empty promises
thinking it could be traded and compensated.

Thinking I could return again later
and make good on all that I swore I would but sometimes,
for all the promises, the realities are just not enough"

...bullshit...

(*I DID'NT APPRECIATE HER WHEN I HAD HER!!!...*)

You are left wishing

(*Will you just listen???*)

Hoping

(*For just 4 minutes???*)

That the front door would just open!!!

That you'd hear the key's jingling and the locks turning
and life would be the same again
and in your heart you know that this time would be different and
that you'd make enough time

MORE than enough!!!!!

For *every five minutes* she needed to confide in you,

You'd give her an **HOUR**

For *every moment* she wanted to be next to you,

You'd give her a **NIGHT FULL**

For *every time* she wanted to see a movie,

You'd give her a **PRODUCTION**

For *every song* she wanted to hear,

You'd choreograph a **SYMPHONY**

For *every time* she missed you,

You'd **BE THERE**

Could she have really found love
in the arms of another?

(*I pray that's ALL it is...*)

Or is it that she has gained her dignity, self-
respect, self-love, and self-motivation enough
to **FINALLY** walk away from **NOTHING**!!!

(*I pray that's* **NOT** *what it is; then I have* **NO** *control...*)

Time ticks

Wishes becoming silent tears

Memories become a silent haunting

Thoughts becoming silent fears

Feelings becoming a silent wanting

(**OHMIGOD**! *This* **CANNOT** *be happening!*)

The clock STILL ticks

(*Baby...*)

And regrets, they follow us so long

Well after she has left

Well after she has moved on

(*I didn't appreciate her when I had her...*)

With tears now running down your closed eyes
you hear the lock turning in the door

(**Baby?!**)

She never even looked back

Chapter VI

Start To Stop...

"Days Like This"

Polished and shined

Wined and dined

Adored by many

Envied by few

Lavished with royalty

Caressed anew

Showered with love

Pampered with joy

Lost in a storm

Ravishing waves that used to lighten your nights now darken your days

Overflowing with the realization

Wishing your heart could be lost

Never knowing what real love can be

Unaware of the burden he's been on you

Battered and bruised

Emotionally tormented

Finally you realize you were unwanted from the beginning

Finding now you're drowning

Leave you reflecting and regretting

...Living...

Days like this

"Can I Have A Few Minutes Of Your Time?"

When I see you, you give
the most gorgeous smile,
masking the frown inside,
you just really want to cry;

You've been hurt so many
times, in so many ways,
over and **OVER** again, and
you just can't seem
to figure out why...

You thought to yourself, the
last guy was the one, I just
KNEW he was fine on the
eyes, money right, dick was
GOOOODDDD, and he
seemed just so **VERY** sweet;

But the more of yourself
you gave to him, the more
you tried, it was **NEVER**
enough, but **MORE** than
enough, to make you
feel **MORE** incomplete...

So now you think, "***MOST
MEN ARE DOGS!***", or maybe
the words were, "***NIGGA'S
AIN'T SHIT!!!!***", after dealing
with just a few;

You've placed a wall around
your heart, reinforced with
steel, and lined with barbed
wire, and refuse to let
anyone through...

And while other men say,
"That's wrong! You shouldn't
be like that baby!"; With
YOU, I totally agree;

Those other men will try to

steal your heart, especially
with that fake sympathy
(You shouldn't be like that
baby!?! LOL!), but a **REAL**
man will have the key...

A **REAL** man won't make you
fall in love, (*He doesn't think
that money, materialism,
good dick, etc will create a
foundation of love in a **REAL**
woman anyway!*) he
leaves that up to you;

His only desire is attaining
and **KEEPING** your trust, **TRUE** happiness,
and in **EVERY** way meaningful,
express his feelings for you,
letting you know what you
REALLY mean to him
in all that he do...

He won't become upset
when you think things are
moving too fast for
WHATEVER reason, and
you want to take it slow...

He knows what you've
been through, knows that
it's hard for you to trust
again, and why, so he
wants to earn the right
to be your man;

When other men think
you're being stuck up, or
playing hard to get, or that
you're making them pay for
another man's mistakes, or,
more often than not, just
cold heatedly say,
"FUCK YOU BITCH!, You
don't have the only pussy
in this world!", a **REAL** man
would understand...

A **REAL** man would never

ask you to "hit it", or "*beat it up*", or "*get in them panties*", or for a "*piece of ass*", or try to be nice (*But **STILL** slick and nasty*) by using a better term like "*make love to him*", or any other terms used to ask you to have sex with him because he knows actions speak louder than words;

He knows that words alone are **NOT** enough; His deeds, and the way he carries them out are what a **REAL** woman pays attention to. This is what **REALLY** arouses a woman, so when the time is right, you'll share your love, especially if he treats you the way you truly deserve...

A **REAL** man is **ALWAYS** able to let you know how much you **REALLY** mean to him and how much he **REALLY** cares for you;

He becomes almost selfish and single minded when it comes to you in a sense, because his only ambition in life is to please you completely, and there's **NOTHING** he wouldn't do...

Maya Angelou called you a "*Phenomenal Woman*", and to me, a reason to disagree has yet to be seen;

Other men call you **EVERYTHING**, from "*Beautiful*" to "*Bitch*", but to **ME** you're simply a **QUEEN**...

So the next time a man walks up and smile, and

wants to know your name;
And he starts to give you
what seems to be the **SAME**
tired ass lines, and what
seems to be the **SAME**
tired ass game...

Tell him, *regardless* of how
good his words sound,
regardless of how good he
looks, *regardless* of how
well he's packaged up, **TELL**
him, "They call me "*QUEEN*",
the "*Phenomenal Woman*",
and my wish should be
your **EVERY** command;

Tell him, *regardless* of the
crazy looks he gives,
regardless of the filthy
words that may emerge
from his mouth, *regardless*
of the unseen, obscene
thoughts in his mind
because of how the clothes
you wear accent your ample
curves and he can't seem to
take his eyes from
your body as you say, "*I'm
the most INCREDIBLE
woman on the face of
the earth, and I don't...*

I WON'T...

Settle for ANYTHING less than a REAL man!"

"Stop The Dance"

He looked at you
and evaluated the
way in which he
would seize you

Calculated all the
right things to
say and do

Gave off an
air of sincerity,
but living
by standards
contradictory of
such beliefs

Loving himself more
than he could
love another, he
came after you

Obtained you;
had you in a
teary eyed state

Had you forgetting
about sweet liberty
and wanting to
be tied in the
shackles that a
relationship demands

Falling into his
net more and
more everyday

All the while being
cognizant, but
not knowing who
you really were

But falling regardless...

You have no
claim in the
person he became;
You just wanted
to keep stock
in his future

But you were
ignorant of the
fact that he
was of the
confused youth

The boys with
the bodies of men
but the mind
of boys still

The boys with
the ages of men
but the maturity
of a boys **STILL**

Not quite a man,
but VERY much a
boy **STILL**!!!

Yes, he was
of the
confused youth

Not knowing
or understanding
which path he
wanted to take

But he *still* sung
his lies of
faithfulness and
truth to you

And you *still*
got caught up
in the harmony
that his
lullabies provided

So when the

songs stopped, you
were left spinning...

Now he climbs on
the highest mountain
to deliver his sermon
of love to another

And you're *still* spinning...

All the while,
your heartbreaks

And you're *still* spinning...

Even though you
put up a facade
to shield yourself
from the pains of
being released, the
walls will still crumble

And you'll **STILL** be spinning...

But thus, that
was his intent

And you surrendered
to the plot submissively

So, once again,
you're left
heartbroken and bruised

Still spinning...

Or are you **REALLY** dancing???

Obviously, there's some

joy you get from
feeling as you do
now because you
CONTINUOUSLY place
yourself in position to
feel as you feel **NOW**

STOP THE DANCE!!!

Chapter VII

Eye/I Empathize, Encourage, and Empower...

"Fellow Men" (All call to love)

Fellow Men...

Look at that woman
and tell her to
look at **HERSELF**...

Not her children
or her husband...

Not at her lack
of abundance or
dire circumstance...

Tell that woman to
stand in front of
the mirror and
look into the
eyes looking back
and take a good
look at **HERSELF**!!!

Fellow Men...

Tell her to look at
her fellow women
and **FEEL** them;
their joy and pain...

Tell her to
close her eyes
and breathe
their air;
their perfumed
presence
in the boardroom
as they work,
or in the basement
as they do
their wash, or
in the schools
as they mold
futures in
the classroom...

Tell her to walk
in their shoes;
Look at herself
in the mirror
and **BE** her
fellow women!!!

Fellow Men...

Lift her up so
that she can
lift up her
fellow woman...

Lift her high
for in
her poverty
is her strength,
in her fear, her
greatest triumph,
in her misfortune,
her determination

Tell her when she
faces the odds,
her strength comes
to maturation and
she takes another
hopeless day or
moment and holds
it close to her
breast to create
the foundation for
a greater future
for those in her
surroundings...

Fellow Men...

Lift her up!!!

Tell her to lift
up that woman
in the mirror!!!

Yes, lift up
that woman
in the street...

In the suburbs
or in the slums...

Let her know
that she's like
life sustaining rain...

Her blood, sweat,
and tears births
and nurtures...

Let that woman
know to remember,
and then remind her
fellow women that
a candle does
not lose its flame
when it lights
another candle...

Fellow Men...

That's called **INSPIRATION**

That's called **ENCOURAGING**

That's called **MOTIVATION**

That's called **EMPOWERING**

Fellow Men...

That's simply **LOVING**
our *fellow women*!!!

"!!!!!NEWSFLASH!!!!!"

!!!!!*NEWSFLASH*!!!!!

On December 18th, 2003, at 8:15 a.m.,
while struggling with the reality
of being a human instead of a myth,
another strong black woman passed away

Medical
sources say
she died of natural
causes, but those who
knew her know she died
from being silent
when she should
have been
screaming

Milling,
when she should
have been raging from
being sick and not wanting
anyone to know because
her pain might
inconvenience
them

She
died from
an overdose
of other people
clinging to her when she
didn't even have
energy for
herself

She
died from
loving men who

didn't love themselves
and could only offer
her a crippled
reflection

She
died from
raising children
alone and for not
being able to do
a complete
job

She
died from
the lies her
grandmother told
her mother and her
mother told **HER** about
life, men &
racism

She
died from
being sexually
abused as a child
and having to take that truth
everywhere she went every day of
her life, exchanging the
humiliation for guilt
and back
again

She
died from
being battered
by someone who
claimed to love her
and she allowed the
battering to go on
to show she
loved him
too

She
died from
asphyxiation,
coughing up blood
from secrets she kept
trying to burn away instead of
allowing herself the kind
of nervous breakdown
she was entitled to,
but only white
girls could
afford

She
died from
being responsible,
because she was the
last rung on the ladder
and there was no one
under her she
could dump
on

Another Strong Black Woman Has Died!!!!!

She
died from
the multiple births of
children she never really wanted
but was forced to have by the
strangling morality of
those around
her

She
died from
being a mother
at 15 and a grandmother
at 30 and an
ancestor at
45

She
died from
being dragged
down and sat upon by
UN-evolved women
posing as
sisters

She
died from
pretending the
life she was
living

Thinking
it was a Kodak
moment instead
of a 20th century,
post-slavery
nightmare

She
died from
tolerating Mr. Pitiful
just to have a man at the
house; just to say that
she had a man
PERIOD!

She
died from
lack of orgasms
because she never learned
what made her body happy and
no one took the time to teach her and
sometimes, when she found arms
that were tender, she died, and
was sometimes re birthed
because they belonged
to the same
gender

She
died from
sacrificing herself for
everybody and everything
when what she really wanted to
do was be a singer, a
dancer, or some
magnificent
other

She
died from
lies of omission
because she didn't
want to bring the
black man
down

She
died from
race memories of being
snatched and raped and snatched
and sold and snatched and bred and
snatched and whipped and snatched
and worked to death and just
SIMPLY snatched at
by the so-called
men of the
present

She
died from
tributes from her
counterparts who should
have been matching her efforts
instead of showering her
with dead words
and empty
songs

She
died from
myths that would
not allow her to show

weakness without being
chastised by the
lazy and
hazy

She
died from
hiding her real
feelings until they
became hard and bitter
enough to invade her
womb and breasts
like angry
tumors

She
died from
always lifting
something; from heavy
boxes and refrigerators to the
lives of men who weren't
strong enough to pick
up themselves,
let alone
her

Another Strong Black Woman Has Died!!!!!

She
died from
the punishments
received from being
honest about life,
racism &
men

She
died from
being called a bitch
for being verbal, a lesbian for
being assertive, and a
whore for picking
her own

lovers

She
died from
never being enough
of what men wanted, or
being **TOO MUCH** for
the men she
wanted

She
died from
being too black
and died again for not
being black
enough

She
died from a
hysterectomy every
time somebody thought
of her as only a woman,
or treated her like
less than a
man

She
died from
being misinformed
about her mind, her body, and
the extent of her royal
capabilities

She
died from
knees pressed too close
together because respect was
never part of the foreplay
that was being
shoved at
her

She
died from
loneliness in birthing
rooms and being alone
in abortion
centers

She
died of
shock in various
courtrooms where she sat, alone,
watching her children
being legally
lynched

She
died in
bathrooms with
her veins busting
open with self-
hatred and
neglect

She
died in
her mind,
fighting life racism
and men, while her body was
carted away and stashed in a
human warehouse for
the spiritually
mutilated

And
sometimes
when she refused
to die, when she just REFUSED
to give in, she was killed by the lethal
images of blond hair , blue eyes
and flat butts, rejected by the
Wesley's, the O.J.'s, the
Quincy 's, & the
Poitiers

Sometimes
she was stomped
to death by racism AND
sexism, executed by hi-tech
ignorance while she carried
the family in her belly,
the community on
her head, and the
race on her
back

Another Strong Black Woman Has Died!!!!!

Or
is she
alive and
kicking?

Must be...

YOU'RE reading this, *right*?????

"My Apology" (For men who can't do it)

Baby, Sexy, Sweetie, Bitch...

Those are **NOT** your name!

We need to stop approaching
you with those bullshit
lines and dumb ass game!

Oh, there **ARE** some of you
that fall for that, and
do whatever we say...

But unless we approach you
like real men, we shouldn't
even be able to come your way.

Because you're a real woman...

It shouldn't be about how big **"IT"**
is, or how *long* we can make it last...

Because whenever you need us
for more than that, you
can't even find our ass!

We've gotten to the point where
we think making you
cum is **ALL** we need to do...

If that was **ALL** you wanted, truth
be told, you can do that yourself,
and you would tell us, "*For that,
I don't even need you!*"

Because you're a real woman...

We should realize that the most
beautiful thing **God** created

stands right before our eyes...

And **YOU** should realize, truth be
told, that "*The Deadliest Weapon
Known To Man*", lies right
between your thighs!

We should **NEVER** stress or wrong
you in **ANY** way because you know
how to use "**IT**", and truth be told, in
so many ways, you know
"**IT**" can make us cry...

You and "**IT**", if you want, **AT THE
LEAST**, can make a husband leave
his wife, a judge turn to a life of
crime, or a pastor tell a lie.

Because you're a real woman...

What we fail to do is learn to
love you, fulfill your dreams, and
at least **TRY** to take
care of **ALL** your needs...

Be **THERE** for you when you **NEED
US MOST**, and our desires you
would surely and happily please.

We need to learn the **TRUE** meaning
of respect, honesty, and trust, and
apply them **CONTINUOUSLY**
when dealing with you...

Act like the **KINGS** we **SHOULD** be,
remain dedicated to making you
happy in **ALL** ways, and performing
the actions and duties of a **QUEEN** to
us will be all that you'd want to do.

Because you're a real woman...

We know, that **YOU** know, that **ALL**
men **ARE NOT** the same, but

the bad ones have made it hard...

Which is why when we approach you,
we shouldn't get upset and disrespect
you like we do, when you
suddenly put up your guard.

Surely, you have the right to protect
yourself from being hurt, we shouldn't
act as if we don't understand...

We need to learn patience, take our
time, and communicate with you
correctly, then maybe you'll
consider letting us be your man.

Because you're a real woman...

I hope my words will let you know
that I **TRULY** empathize and
understand exactly how you feel...

And to reassure you, because I
understand why you no longer believe,
that someone who's more than a man, a
GENTLEMAN, actually exists and is real.

So to **YOU** who's reading this, striving
to become more than a
woman, the **LADY** you want to be...

I implore you to **NEVER**, **EVER**, give up
on your hopes and dreams, compromise
or debase yourself in **ANY WAY AT ALL** for
NO man, and more importantly, stay true
to **YOURSELF**, as well as what YOU believe!

Because you should be **MORE** than a *real woman*...

You should be a **TRUE LADY**!!!

"!!!!!NEWSFLASH!!!!! Pt. 2"

(The confessions of the bad black man)

Have a seat sister; this may take a while. Don't be afraid. The two pistols you see smoking in my hands are harmless now. Both clips are empty, much like a *George Bush* or *Hilary Clinton* speech. And even though I was aiming at the "*System*" when I first unloaded shots into the air, I see now that I missed the target. The "*System*" remains intact while you sit wounded and battle-weary from decades of bullets being lodged deep into your heart and soul

I murdered you many times. Still, you didn't die; Not even once.

I apologize for abandoning you and leaving you to fend for yourself in a world as cruel as it is cold. I should have supported you when you offered to be a part of the struggle. But the struggle was an internal one as well as an external one, and I was losing on both fronts. I became angered at you for straightening your hair, for slow dancing in the arms of white men, for challenging my manhood and comparing it to other races. I hated the way the "*System*" divided us by promoting you and demoting me, but instead of uniting with you and having your back, I attacked you and left you alone in your grief

I murdered you many times. Still, you didn't die; Not even once.

I apologize for flaunting white women in your face as soon as I got money or fame. I was suffering from a mental illness that had me believing that my self-worth had to be approved by blue eyes. I know it hurt you to see me betray you so quickly, so easily, and so often. I had you feeling as though you were not worthy to be in my arms when the opposite was true: **I** was **NOT** worthy to be in the arms of *yours*

I murdered you many times. Still, you didn't die; Not even once.

I apologize for calling you a "*bitch*" and a "*hoe*" and treating you like a sexual object in my music, in my poetry, in the streets, in my speech, and amongst my homeboys. I felt powerless and frustrated, lost in a maze of self-hatred. I raped you, and pimped you, and beat you, and cursed you, and tried to destroy you in the same way I felt destroyed. The pressures of society triggered the implosion that almost destroyed everything inside of me. And you got caught up in the blast because you were always so determined to stand firmly by my side

I murdered you many times. Still, you didn't die: Not even once.

I apologize for cheating on you, abusing you, and leaving you as soon as you got pregnant. I pretended like the child wasn't mine. I even asked you to kill the baby because I knew I wasn't responsible enough to rear him/her properly. When you refused, I reluctantly tossed you a few dollars each month and felt like that's all I had to do to be a father. I apologize for turning you into a single mother instead of a happy wife

I murdered you many times. Still, you didn't die: Not even once.

I apologize for selling drugs and going to prison and using the streets as an excuse for my failure. I didn't want to be like the honest folks in my hood who worked hard and had nothing to show for it. I wanted more out of life but didn't have the courage or the insight to follow the path of the brothers who worked hard in school to build stable futures and lives for themselves. I grew up angry at the world and my environment. But instead of using this anger in a constructive manner, I beat down and shot up the first brother who stepped on my shoes in the club

I murdered you many times. Still, you didn't die: Not even once.

I apologize for dying so young in the streets. I just wanted respect. I just wanted power. And the only people in my hood who possessed these qualities were the gangsters and thugs and dealers. You warned me to be careful. You begged me to slow down. But I didn't listen. The respect of the street was all I had. It was something I was willing to kill for, to even die for. I was fighting a war against myself, and dying for a cause that didn't exist

I murdered you many times. Still, you didn't die; Not even once.

I apologize for breaking your heart and betraying your trust and hurting you so badly that you became almost as racist as the "System". You started calling all black men dogs and writing cruel little "Waiting to Exhale" type books that spent too much time degrading me instead of explaining how good black men could REALLY be a majority. Your anger and books flew high, like an eagle, towards the tree branches of my soul. But instead of forgiving me and attempting to rebuild your nest, your anger and books became woodpeckers that pecked away at what was left of me, and made good black men a minority

I murdered you many times. Still, you didn't die; Not even once.

You screamed out that good black men were hard to find and blamed me for your actions when you held white men in your arms. I tried to tell you that I was the minority, and that good black men were everywhere, but it was easier for you to point fingers at me than it was to give these brothers a chance. I should have treated you like the queen that you are so that other good black men wouldn't be falsely accused of my emotional crimes

I murdered you many times. Still, you didn't die; Not even once.

I apologize for encouraging you to be materialistic. I dumped my money into the same "System" that was destroying me and tried to impress you with expensive cars, platinum jewelry, and Coogi gear. I fooled you into thinking that the measure of a man was in the size of his bank account or in the size of the knot in his front pocket or in the size of his penis, disregarding the size of my ego. You jumped into the front seat of my Lexus, happy because your friends were now envious of you, as we both sped down a dead end road at one hundred miles per hour. As a result, many good black men who didn't own a Lexus were ignored and even dismissed by you. I had you believing that your love came with a price tag

I murdered you many times. Still, you didn't die; Not even once.

I apologize for the late night booty calls. You wanted to talk, to cuddle, and to explore the depth of my character. I only wanted sex. I called you when I was horny and only reached out to you when I saw that you were slipping away. I should have talked to you and opened up to you. Instead, I trusted only my homeboys and factored you out of the equation

I murdered you many times. Still, you didn't die; Not even once.

And I apologize for turning you against your friends and family members. I was jealous of their influence over you. I was afraid that you would listen to them when they told you that I was not good for you. I didn't have a job, and when I did, I used it as a weapon against you. When wise sisters told you to raise your standards, I persuaded you to lower them. I had you thinking that you had to have a man, any man, to be complete. And I apologize for that

I murdered you MANY times, sister

Yet, **INCREDIBLY, AMAZINGLY,** you **DIDN'T** die

NOT EVEN ONCE!!!!!

And this serves as the **ULTIMATE TESTIMONY** to your **TRUE GREATNESS AND WORTH**

"You Will Survive"

You wish to survive

And save the
broken pieces
for later

Because all
tomorrow's hopes
and dreams
were made for
this moment

You're hiding deep

Moving slow,
because that
sweet kiss
you always
lusted for
was mixed
with sour wine
and seemingly
waited for no
one but you

You will survive

Love is patient

It knows its
own reflection
hungers for those
special moments

Twined in
your heart

More stubborn
than you

You will survive

Lady of Grace

Goddess of Love

Queen of Desire

Beauty of Dreams

You were lulled
asleep by
his false love

You were kissed
by him thru
the heart where
his brutish
arrow struck

But with it's
painful penetration
you're **NOW** awake!

For you are
more worthy
than this

His
meaningless
kiss

His hugs, empty
claims of love and
insignificant promises

Superficial-language-
to-hold-onto-to-you-
but-don't-really-
want-you **BULLSHIT**

You **WILL** survive

The mists of
the pains of
packaged love

You **WILL** survive

They were **NEVER**
meant for you

That terrible
excuse of
a man

That horrible
glowing apparition
of a man
which all
others somehow
paled to

He out shined
the rest to
shed blinding, yet
superficial light
on you only
to place you
in darkness

But you **WILL** survive

Even after you've
tasted his
venomous tongue

Even after you
became inseminated
by his poisonous penis

Even after you
haphazardly climbed
with him to places
no woman was
NEVER meant
to ascend

You **WILL** survive

You'll fly to new crests

Leaving nothingness beneath

Your justice awaits you
You have a
soul that could
NEVER be denied

A spirit that
could **NEVER** die

You **WILL** survive

You'll remain in
hold of
your passions

In control of
your actions

Like the green
in a new
shoot of grass

You'll grow

You **WILL** survive

In wandering lost
you'll find yourself

A Queen **WILL**
find herself

Your dominion
is your own
as so it
always should be

You are **NOT**
in the flavor
of the hunted

You are in
favor of the
blessed and
anointed

You **ARE** wanted

Passionately desired
But **NO LONGER**
a prey of man

You're a **SURVIVOR**

You'll be sought
by the man
who seeks to
see your eyes
shine in his

Watch you in
his arms dance
free and **NOT**
entrap you in his

He'll know your
heart because his
beats for **YOU**

He'll know the
adversities, struggles,
and wrongdoings
you've endured
and will **HELP**
you survive as
opposed to being
another man
you've survived from

Yes

YOU WILL SURVIVE!!!

Made in the USA
Charleston, SC
26 February 2010